Tell Us About The
Holy Spirit, Papa

Written by Tom Mullenix

Illustrated by Gene Dearing

7710-T Cherry Park Dr, Ste 224
Houston, TX 77095
www.WorldwidePublishingGroup.com

The views expressed in this book are the author's and do not necessarily reflect those of the publisher.

Illustrated by Gene Dearing

Published in the United States of America.

Softcover: 978-1-68411-103-9
Hardcover: 978-1-68411-127-5

Acknowledgements

This book is dedicated to my grandchildren:

Jarin, Brooks, Claire, Karlie, Kyle, Elise, Caleb, Emerson and Lydia.

My gratitude to:

- Laura, my wife and their Nana. She has shared her skills as an author to coach me through this project. Her encouragement is priceless.

- Gene Dearing whose artwork you will see throughout the book. Our friendship was forged by the Spirit of God.

Table of Contents

Introduction

I am so happy that you want to follow Jesus! Living for Jesus can be a lot of fun. Sometimes living for Jesus can be very hard.

That is because Jesus asks us to do some things that are difficult. Some very sad and frustrating things can happen in our lives. Jesus always planned for you and me to have help while we live for him. BIG HELP.

A little more than a month after Jesus rose from the dead, he left the earth and went to heaven. He's staying there until the time for him to come back and bring us home with him.

After Jesus went to heaven, he sent the Holy Spirit here to live with everyone who obeys Jesus. The Holy Spirit is the BEST HELPER you can ever have.

I have written this book to introduce you to the Holy Spirit and describe for you all the ways that he can help you.

I am a grandfather. My nine grandchildren call me "Papa." I have been a church pastor for a long,

long time (40 years) and also a missionary. I have learned, myself, how to team up with the Holy Spirit. Then I wrote to my older grand kids to help them live for Jesus. Now I am writing to you.

You can read through the book quickly; but you can also slow down and study each idea.

I have listed for you a lot of scriptures that you can look up and study for yourself. I have taken time to explain some things more carefully so you can understand well.

You will find some extra information in *footnotes*. From time to time, while you are reading, you'll see a little number next to a word or sentence. Look down at the bottom of the page and you'll see that number again – with extra information.

I want you to get to know the Holy Spirit really well. Not so you can pass a test or show off with your answers; but so you and the Spirit of God can be great teammates.

Given to

_____

Given by

_____

Date _____

CHAPTER 1
Something special

Something very special happened when you were baptized. God moved into you. His name is the Holy Spirit. Did you feel anything different? It is ok if you didn't. Jesus promised that he would come and Jesus always keeps his promises. He said the Holy Spirit would live with us and be in us.[1]

On the first day that anyone ever became a Christian, they were all told to change their minds and be baptized. The Bible word for changing your mind is "repent." When they did that, their sins would be forgiven and they would receive a special gift – the Holy Spirit.[2] A lot of people decided to be baptized that day; do you know how many? Three Thousand! Just in one day! But that was no problem for God. The Holy Spirit was able to move into each of them. He is that powerful and he is really awesome!

It is hard for us to understand a spirit, because we can't see one. There are other things that we can't see,

---

[1] John 14:15-17

[2] Acts 2:38

yet they are very real; can you name any of them? (How about wind? Sound? Atoms? Germs?) Each of them is real and a part of our lives each day.

Jesus talked to a man named Nicodemus about this.[3] Jesus told him about the wind; he said that we can't really see wind; and Jesus is right, you know. What do we see? We see how the wind pushes things around like trees and flags and the paper that you need to pick up! We see what the wind does, but we cannot see the actual wind. Jesus said that we will be able to see what the Holy Spirit does in our lives, but we won't see him.

By the way, in both the Hebrew and Greek languages the word we translate "spirit" means spirit, breath or wind. The Old Testament was written in Hebrew and the New in the Greek language.

When the Bible tells us how God created the first man, it says that he formed him out of the dirt and breathed into his nostrils the breath of life – and he came alive[4]. You and I are just like Adam, we have a

---

[3] John 3:5-8

[4] Genesis 2:7

spirit.   We are like God that way – because he is Spirit.[5]

We are a spirit who lives inside our body. We are used to it. We don't think about being a spirit, just like we don't often think about breathing, unless we are having problems with asthma or a bad cold, right?

So the Holy Spirit is now inside of you. He is living with your spirit and you won't feel him, just like you don't normally feel yourself breathing. You won't see him, just like you can't really see the wind. But, you can know he is there because he is now inside you to do a very, very important job.

He has moved inside of you to help you as you live for Jesus![6]

---

[5] John 4:24

[6] Ezekiel 36:26, 27

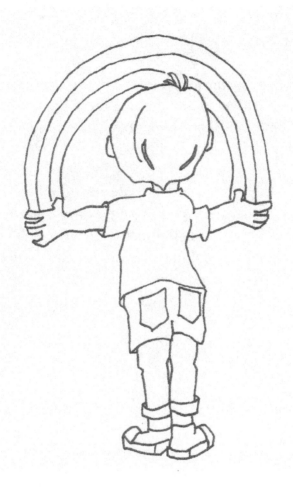

14

CHAPTER 2
To help you live for Jesus

The Holy Spirit has moved inside of you to help you as you live for Jesus!

The Holy Spirit is God. He is not the Father or the Son – Jesus; but he is God. We can talk about that more sometime. Jesus said that the Holy Spirit is just like him.[7]   Here's how I know that – the New Testament was written in the Greek language. In that language, they had two ways of saying "another."

If I fixed you an ice cream sundae with vanilla ice cream, hot fudge, sprinkles and whipped cream – I think you would like that, wouldn't you? – Then, if the next day I asked, "Do you want **another** sundae?" You could tell me, "Yes, but I want chocolate ice cream, marshmallows & a cherry." Is that the same sundae? No.

In Greek, you can say that – "I want another; a different kind." Or you can say, "I want another, the same kind." You can say that with just one word!

---

[7] John 14:15-17

Jesus called the Holy Spirit another Counselor.[8]   He said **another** *of the same kind.* In other words, he said, "The Holy Spirit is just like me."[9]

Jesus also called the Holy Spirit a word in Greek that means too much to say in just one English word. He called the Holy Spirit our: Counselor, Friend, Helper, Lawyer, Comforter and Assistant – all of those! Jesus used the Greek word "paraclete." (The word sounds like those little green & yellow birds that people keep in cages; or like two shoes that baseball players wear.) It means "someone who comes right beside you so he can help you."

The Holy Spirit can help us because he is just like Jesus. When we need to understand something, he will help us think. When we are lonely, he will let us know that God loves us. When we need to tell someone the truth, he will help us to not lie. When we are sad, he will let us know that God cares about our sadness. He is always here to help us. He is inside you and me – don't ever forget.

---

[8] John 14:16

[9] He is so much like Jesus, that sometimes in the New Testament he is called the Spirit of Jesus. Acts 16:6, 7 is one place

One of his main jobs is to help us obey Jesus. *"I will put my Spirit in you. I will move you to follow my rules. I want you to be careful to keep my laws."* Ezekiel 36:27 (New International Readers Version)

You and I were baptized[10] because we wanted to follow Jesus and to please him with what we do, think and say. The Holy Spirit wants to help. He is strong enough to be the best Helper, but he will not force you to obey Jesus. What he will do is encourage you to think about and do the right things. After that, when you decide to obey Jesus, he will give you extra strength to do it well.

---

[10] Acts 9:17, 18; Acts 19:1-6; Acts 5:32; Titus 3:3-8; Acts 2:38. These are verses that talk about the Holy Spirit and baptism.

CHAPTER 3

The Holy Spirit really helps us

Get your Bible and find the book of Romans in the New Testament. I want to show you three very good things that the Holy Spirit does for us.

In Romans 15:13, Paul is writing a prayer asking God to do nice things for the Christians who are reading his letter – that's you and me, too! We are Christians reading his letter.

Go ahead and read the verse: Do you see what it tells us about God? He is the God of hope – we can always look forward to something good when we live for God. When we trust God he will give us a lot of joy and peace – we will be full.

Then what will the Holy Spirit do for us? How much hope will we have? So much that it will be spilling out of you! Did you ever fill a cup or bucket with so much water that you couldn't move it without it spilling? That is what the Holy Spirit will do in your life – he will give you so much hope that you will spill hope on people when they bump you!

Now find Romans chapter 5 and read some more verses. Read verses 3, 4 & 5. (When people write Bible verses to read, they will write that as Romans 5:3-5.) Take time to read it right now. This tells us about times in our lives when things go wrong: like when we are hurt or sick, or when someone is mean to us. There are also times when we do something wrong and are facing the consequences. God does not leave us when bad things happen. He wants to use those times to help us grow up.

Do you see what happens during times when we suffer? We learn to try again and not give up (perseverance). We stop doing the bad thing and learn to do better. This is called "character." You can ask your Mom or Dad about that word.

And there is hope again! God likes for us to look forward to the good things he will do in our lives. The Holy Spirit is mentioned again in verse 5. What is he going to do for us? Does that sound like he is going to give us a little bit of God's love, or a lot?

I have had bad things happen in my life and I know that these verses are true. In my life, the Holy

Spirit has done two things – he helped me to feel God's love for me and he helped me to love God more. I am thankful for the way the Holy Spirit helps me when I am suffering. He will help you, too.

One more place to look – find Romans 8. Read verses 5 and 6. Your Bible may say 'sinful nature' or 'flesh' in verse 5 – let me help you understand what that means.

The Bible talks about a rebellious and bad attitude that is inside each of us. You know how your parents tell you to do something or to stop doing something and part of you wants to disobey? We all struggle with that.

When you were baptized, God made that rebellious part of you weaker[11], it can't force you anymore, but it still invites you to do bad things! I have the same experience, even though I am much older than you.

Pay attention to what these verses say, they are very important for us to understand. It matters what you choose to put in your mind. You and I want to live to make the Holy Spirit happy, so we are going to

---

[11] Romans 6:6; Colossians 2:11, 12

think about the things that please him. Since the Holy Spirit wrote the Bible[12] one of the best things we can do is read the Bible and learn memory verses.

What happens to you when the Holy Spirit controls your mind? What happens to you when your old naughty attitude controls your mind?

It is really important to be careful what you watch on TV and movies, and what you see in video games. It is important to pay attention to what you talk about with friends and what you read about because many times they can encourage us to do things that disobey God.

It is hard sometimes to say "no," because it seems like those things are really fun. If you think a lot about these things, it will hurt you inside and can push you away from God.[13] It is important that you block bad thoughts from getting into your mind and put the thoughts the Holy

---

[12] There will be more about this in chapter 11.

[13] Death means "separation." When someone dies, their spirit leaves their body. That is separation. A person can be dead in their spirit, even if their body is alive by being separated from God. God wants us to live with him as his friend and child.

Spirit gives[14] into your mind. Then you will really, really enjoy life.

Let's add up what we've learned here in Romans: life and peace, joy and hope and learning to know and feel God's love – these all come from the Holy Spirit as we obey God and let him work in our lives. The Holy Spirit has done these things in my life and I hope you will be able to tell others how he has helped you.

---

[14] They will be from the Bible. Learn the Bible, especially about Jesus and the New Testament. The Holy Spirit will help you to remember the right things when you fill your mind with God's Word.

CHAPTER 4

The Holy Spirit keeps on helping us

Are you ready for some more Bible study about the Holy Spirit? I hope so. He is the one who will help us live for Jesus and obey Jesus. The Holy Spirit moved inside of us when we were baptized to prove that we belong to Jesus.[15]

Get your Bible ready. I want to show you three places where the Holy Spirit does really good things in our lives. Find Ephesians 3:16, 17. Go ahead and read those verses now. Paul wrote down a prayer for the Christians he knew. That prayer is a good one for us to pray for each other. What did Paul ask in his prayer? He prayed that the Holy Spirit would make us very strong on the inside!

We all like superheroes; it is fun to see how they beat the bad guys. They have special powers and are very strong. But they are also just stories, they aren't real. It is very good to have strong bodies, but it is even more important to be strong inside: in our

---

[15] Ephesians 1:13, 14; Galatians 4:6, 7

hearts, souls, character (Remember? You were going to ask your Mom or Dad about that word). The Holy Spirit will help us to especially be strong inside. Now, look at verse 17 again.

The Holy Spirit has a special reason for making us strong. Do you see it? It's so Jesus can live in us. Hold it, I thought the Holy Spirit lived in us and Jesus is in heaven. Remember earlier I told you that the Holy Spirit is just like Jesus? They are so much alike that when the Spirit lives in us, it is just the same as Jesus being there.

The big thing I want you to think about is this – the Holy Spirit wants to work in us so that Jesus will be at home in our lives. You know how you like to have your things just right, just the way you want them to be? And you get upset sometimes when someone messes them up? Do you know how it feels after you have been away for a long time and you get back to your home?

Jesus wants to feel that way with you, and he wants you to feel that way with him. He wants us to feel at home with him – comfortable with Jesus and wanting to be with Jesus every day, like he is part of the family. If you feel that way about Jesus now, good! If you had not thought about it, tell God that you want Jesus to feel at home in you. Tell him that you want the Holy Spirit to help prepare you.

Now turn a page or maybe two and go to Ephesians 5:18. Many times in the Bible we are told, "Don't do this bad thing," instead "Do this good thing." This verse says just that: you can talk with your Mom or Dad about the first part (the "don't do"). You and I will talk about the second part. What does it tell us to do? That's right, be filled with the Spirit.

Some people are bigger than others; does that mean they get more Holy Spirit so they can be full? No, the same Holy Spirit lives in each of us. He can do this because he is God. You and I are "filled" with the Holy Spirit when we give him permission to be involved in every part of our lives.

Did you know that some people don't want that? They want the Holy Spirit to go with them to church so they can feel good when they sing. Also, so everyone will like them and think they are really good Christians. But they do not want the Holy Spirit with them at home, or when they are thinking about doing something bad, or when they are with their friends.

They don't want the Holy Spirit to show them how to obey Jesus. They just want him to help them to feel good and look good. So it is kind of like putting the Holy Spirit in your bedroom closet and locking the door. And you only let him out when you go to church!

The Holy Spirit comes into our lives to help us obey Jesus, but he won't force us to obey. We need to cooperate; we need to tell him that he has permission to work on every part of our lives. The best way I know to do this is to pray and ask God, "Fill me with the Holy Spirit."

I do this every day. An old time preacher named Dwight Moody prayed this prayer a lot. His friend asked, "Why do you ask to be filled by the Spirit so much?" Moody said, "It is because I leak!" I leak, too, and so I have learned to ask to be filled every day. Why don't you to try it?

The last place I want to show you is Galatians 5:22, 23. Find it in your Bible and read it. Here are the words from the NIRV, *"But the fruit the Holy Spirit produces is love, joy and peace. It is being patient, kind and good. It is being faithful and gentle and having control of oneself* (that means – you! Self-control). *There is no law against things of that kind."*

These verses tell us that we are the Holy Spirit's garden. We are like a tree, bush or plant and the Holy Spirit wants to grow good things in us. What is your favorite fruit? Does it come from a tree, bush or plant? What about your favorite vegetable? Ok, one that you can stand eating if you have to?

When we let the Holy Spirit work in us, when we don't lock him in a closet, lots of good attitudes and actions start to grow in us. Like in a garden, they grow slowly. Sometimes you can't tell a change is happening, but then you see it – the fruit is getting bigger, someday soon it will be ready.

Talk with your Mom or Dad about the list of things that the Holy Spirit wants to grow in you. Are you doing some of them well? Could they be better or bigger in you? Are there some that you have a really hard time with? I want to encourage you to pray about them. Tell God that you really want these attitudes – because you want to be like Jesus – and ask that the Holy Spirit would help you grow them in your life.

Remember, it is the Holy Spirit's job to make them grow. It is your job to let him know that you want to be like Jesus. Keep reading your Bible, and praying about this. There is another garden verse in

Galatians[16]. Maybe you can read it with your parents or grandparents. When you read your Bible, learn memory verses and try to obey God's Word, you are planting (sowing) to please the Spirit[17].

---

[16] Galatians 6:7, 8

[17] Just like we talked about in Romans 8:5, 6

CHAPTER 5

The Conflict

It was a great day when the Holy Spirit moved into you.[18] Your family was happy. People who know you encouraged you. I remember when I was baptized (I was eleven) – I felt both relieved and happy. Maybe you felt like that, too.

But not everyone was happy that day: the devil was mad because you broke away from his power – now you belong to God.[19]

Something inside you was not happy either – your sinful nature. Your Bible may call it "flesh" but it is not talking about your skin. **Your sinful nature wasn't happy at all that the Holy Spirit moved into your life.**

Do you remember when we talked about this? Your sinful nature, or flesh, is a mixture of the bad attitudes, bad habits and the desire to rebel that is inside you. Have you noticed how little kids do the

---

[18] Chapter 1.

[19] Acts 26:17, 18

opposite of what you tell them to do? We all have some of that inside us – we rebel.

When I tell you that your sinful nature was not happy, I mean it was MAD. It was not willing to be quiet or share. You can see what's coming … there is going to be a fight.

I remember when we moved to Hawaii many years ago. Our boys were in the 1st and 4th grade. They were different.   Most kids were Asian or Hawaiian – they had black hair and dark eyes and darker skin.

When someone is different, often the other kids pick on them. Is this something that you have seen? Our boys got into some fights, often just because they were different and the others didn't want to accept them. (You will be glad to know that eventually they made friends there and everything was fine.)

That is kind of like what happens inside of us when we become Christians. Our sinful nature starts a fight with the Holy Spirit. Paul talks about it this way – *"The sinful nature wants to do evil, which is just the opposite of what the Spirit wants. And the Spirit gives us desires that are the opposite of what the sinful nature* desires. *These two forces are constantly fighting each other, so you are not free to carry out your good intentions."*[20]

So, here we are – Christians who love Jesus, and there is this fight going on inside of us. And it's not some video game; it is serious. The Bible also says that sinful desires fight a war against our souls.[21]

The apostle Paul talks about how frustrating this is in the book of Romans.[22] He said, "I want to do good things, but I keep doing bad things." "There is this struggle or contest going on inside me and I feel like I am losing."

I understand how Paul felt. I remember after I was baptized that I wanted to change and live in a way that would please Jesus (I told you how old I was, do you remember?). I did change in a lot of ways, but I certainly struggled with picking on my sisters (I have three sisters and I am bigger than they are). I would decide that I was going to stop and I would pray and ask God to help me stop. Soon, I was picking on them again, and we would be fighting.

---

[20] Galatians 5:17 (New Living Translation)

[21] 1 Peter 2:11

[22] Romans 7:14-25

Sometimes it is very hard to stop doing bad things. It seems like doing those things might be fun – the devil wants us to think that way. But if you ever talk to someone who has listened to the devil and has done the things that Jesus tells us to stay away from – they will tell you that it stops being fun, they have many bad feelings and bad memories.

Sometimes it is like we have someone or something pushing us to do stuff that is wrong. We do. Paul was so frustrated he said, "What a terrible failure I am!"[23] Then he said, "Who can help me?" His answer? "Thank God – Jesus our Lord will help us!"

Have you felt the fight inside of you? If you have, I want you to understand that this is normal. I will explain in the next chapter how to face this fight. If you have not experienced this trouble, I want you to understand that you will. And when you do feel it – don't be afraid, God has not left you. He wants us to learn how to stand strong for Jesus.

I will explain next how the Holy Spirit is ready to help you and me. He wants to be our coach, our

---

[23] Romans 7:24 (New International Readers Version)

friend and our power supply – it will be smart to accept his offer of help.

CHAPTER 6
Winning the Conflict

We were talking about the battle, the fight that is going on inside of us: our rebellious, bad attitude fighting against the Holy Spirit. It can be very frustrating.

Why does God let that happen? Why doesn't he just take that bad attitude and throw it away? I don't know why. I do know that it would be a lot easier if he did, but our Heavenly Father has decided that this is a way to make us strong.

Let me show you something from the Old Testament.[24] Do you remember when Joshua led the armies of Israel to conquer the bad guys and take over their Promised Land? You can read it in the book of Joshua. They won some great battles and God helped them with some miracles. They pushed the bad kings and their armies far enough away that God's people could move in and have their own land.

---

[24] Judges 3:1-4

But each group from Israel (they were called tribes) was responsible to finish driving the bad guys out of their land. We are told the reason why in chapter three of Judges – God wanted the young people to learn how to fight in war. Think about that. It was important to God that his people would know how to stand up to the bad guys and defeat them! The same thing is true for both you and me.

This time, the bad guys are not people; instead they are bad attitudes and sinful problems. These are dangerous because we can't see them (they are inside us) and they can cause us to forget to live for Jesus.

The Holy Spirit can help us fight these battles – we can be like superheroes[25] when we work with him! I have already given you some scriptures about how the Holy Spirit helps us.

When we think about the things that belong to the Holy Spirit[26] he gives us life and peace. Some of those things are scripture verses and praise songs. When we take time to do things to make the Holy Spirit happy he helps us to experience eternal life. It's

---

[25] Remember – in chapter 4 I told you that superheroes are just stories. Our life with the Holy Spirit is real.

[26] Romans 8:5-8

like we are planting a garden in our hearts[27] by doing what Jesus tells us to do; both good attitudes and doing good things.

Think about this – eternal life is not just when we go to heaven; it is when we live with Jesus today – every day, all the time.[28]

Now I want you to really pay attention here. I never learned this when I was young, and so I didn't realize what power was available to me. I am telling you because I want you to know how much power you have to win this fight!

The Holy Spirit is able to kill our bad attitudes and sinful habits. He wants to do it, but he is waiting for us to ask for help. How do I know that? Because that is what I read in scripture.

Look up Romans 8 in your Bible. Romans 8:9-11 tell us how very important it is that the Holy Spirit lives in you and me. What do you see there? Why is this so important?

---

[27] Galatians 6:7-10

[28] John 17:3; 1 Thessalonians 5:9, 10

Then the next three verses (8:12-14) talk about how the Holy Spirit works inside you and me to win battles. It says we have an obligation (that's a duty, something we have to do or something we owe to someone). We do not have to live for our rebellious attitudes. In fact, if we do, we will die – this is serious stuff!

Do you see how the Holy Spirit helps us? The best way for me to explain this is have you think about bugs or mice or snakes. Does your mom like them? Does she want them in her house? I don't think that you would enjoy a lot of them in the house, I know I wouldn't. And once they get into your house, they like it there and don't want to leave. So what can we do?

We have to find a way to close up where they are coming in and, then, to kill the ones inside. That may sound mean, but it is the only way. We may have to hire someone who is an expert to do it for us. That person is called an exterminator.

We have the same problem with our rebellious attitude and bad habits. I am not talking about biting our nails, but the ones that the Bible tells us are sin. At times, no matter how hard we try, they just won't go away. These verses tell us that the Holy Spirit will kill them. Yes, he will kill them if we ask him to do it. We really have to want these bad things to be gone – because if you don't take it seriously, you will be blocking the Holy Spirit as he works.

I'm going to tell you how the Holy Spirit helped me: I had a bad habit that was really hurting someone I love very much. I would get mad and argue – I was really mean. I was loud and my voice was mean. When she was trying to tell me something, I would butt in and argue. I tried very hard to stop it, because I knew it was hurting her, but I could not. I wanted to change! I wanted to stop this bad attitude!

So I took these verses (Romans 8:12-14) and I prayed that the Holy Spirit would kill this bad stuff in me. And slowly, he began to change me. A little at a time, I got better. I began to stop doing it as much. I caught myself before I got started. I apologized for arguing much sooner. Every day I asked the Holy Spirit step in and kill my bad habit. Each day, I got a little better. I am not perfect, but I am different. The days I forget to pray, I make more mistakes. The Holy Spirit is helping me!

He wants to help you, too. He wants to lead you to change your attitudes and actions so that you will please Jesus.

Now, it is not just the Holy Spirit's job to do alone. We can't tell him, "Kill that," and go watch TV. We are to work together with him. There is another place in the Bible that tells us to kill the bad attitudes and sins in us.[29] So, you see, we're a team: The Holy Spirit and me or the Holy Spirit and you. We work together to obey Jesus and to get rid of the bad things we think, do and say.

When you invite the Holy Spirit to help you, the power of God will be working in your life. Always remember that.

---

[29] Colossians 3:5; read all of these verses – Colossians 3:5-11

CHAPTER 7

Walk in the Spirit

The Holy Spirit has moved into you and me to help. He wants to help us to please Jesus by the way we live every day.[30]

I have found four commands concerning our teamwork with the Holy Spirit in your New Testament – a command is "YOU DO THIS". Two of the commands are, "Be sure to do this!" and two are, "You don't want to go there."

We need to study carefully so we can obey these commands. It will help if you get your Bible ready.

"Walk in the Spirit."[31] Does the Holy Spirit have his own brand of walking shoes? Maybe your Bible says, "Live by the Spirit." Remember when the Bible was written, they did not have cars or motorcycles or even scooters. Most people didn't even own a horse

---

[30] By the way, we don't have to fear making Jesus upset. He always loves us. He does not like sin. He also knows what is best for us. It's when we please Jesus that we are truly happy ourselves.

[31] Galatians 5:16, 18, 25

or donkey, they had to walk anywhere that they wanted to go. So "walk" meant – live your life.

Come to think of it, I walk many places that I go. I never drive my car in the house. Miss Laura (my wife) wouldn't like that! I walk for exercise. I walk in the grocery store. I walk when I am shopping. I bet you walk a lot, too.

It is a normal thing to walk. "Walk in the Spirit" (or "live by the Spirit") tells us that teamwork with the Holy Spirit should be as normal as walking into the kitchen when you want a snack. The Holy Spirit is ready to help us to follow Jesus closely. He is waiting for you and me. When we want to cooperate with him and live for Jesus, he will help us big time.

He'll help you to stand up to your rebellious attitude and tell it "No! Enough!"[32] And he will teach you how to truly love your family and other Christians.[33]

The Holy Spirit will help change the way you think – from "I'm doing this because I must" to "I'm

---

[32] Galatians 5:16. Gratify means to satisfy or make happy. So this verse means that we won't care to help our rebellious attitudes.

[33] Galatians 5:13

doing this because I want to."[34]   I think that you would agree with me, it is more fun to do something because you want to do it. The Holy Spirit can help us make hard things in life easier, when we let him help us change the way we think.

One more – we need to act like we are in the army or in a marching band with the Holy Spirit. We need to "keep in step with the Spirit."[35] Have you seen people march together? If you haven't, maybe you can find it on youtube. It's really interesting, unless they are marching out of step, then it's a mess (unless you are watching the Three Stooges … that's funny).

You have to practice a lot to stay 'in step' together. This means that we need to practice living with the Holy Spirit, practice our teamwork by obeying Jesus.

If you are reading your Bible every day and praying that you can learn to do these things, the Holy Spirit can do his part and give you extra power to please Jesus.

---

[34] Galatians 5:18. The idea of a law is "you have to obey it."

[35] Galatians 5:25

CHAPTER 8

Don't put out the
Spirit's fire

Now we come to the "Don't go there" command.[36] "Don't put out the Spirit's fire."

Fire can cause a lot of trouble. It can burn down houses and other buildings. That's why we have fire departments. To stop that trouble. Do you live near a fire station?

But fire can also provide good things. When it is cold in the winter, fire heats your house. Do you like to take cold showers? Fire heats the water for your shower or bath. (Ask your Dad or Mom to tell you how furnaces or water heaters work.) Often people use fire to cook food. Do you like hotdogs or hamburgers that have been cooked on the grill?

When fire is burning down a house, it is good that the firemen fight that fire. When fire is doing good

------

[36] 1 Thessalonians 5:19 Some Bible versions say, "Do not quench the Spirit."

things, like cooking your hot dog, it is a mistake to put out that fire.

There are really a lot of ways to put out a fire, can you think of some? See how many you can think of, then look at my ideas at the bottom of the page – **don't look until you make a list**.[37]

Fire needs fuel (like wood, charcoal or paper) and oxygen (that is already in the air). Using an extinguisher or water stops oxygen for a moment, then they make it harder for the fuel to burn.

Now, we know a lot about fires – what about the Holy Spirit? I'm going to use a good Bible Study word – **context**. Context means to read the verses before and after to see what the writer is talking about. This context is from verse 12 all the way to verse 22 (1 Thessalonians 5:12-22).

There we learn a lot of ways to be kind and help people. It also tells us that both praying and telling God "thank you" are some things we should do a lot. Then, "don't put out the Spirit's fire." After that, we

---

[37] Put out a fire? 1) Pour water on it. 2) Use a fire extinguisher. 3) Smother the fire with a blanket or towel.   4) Remove the oxygen from the room. 5) Remove the fuel for the fire. 6) Call the fire department. *How many were on your list?*

are told not to have a bad attitude about people who teach us God's Word.[38]

But we also need to be careful.[39] Just because a teacher tells us something doesn't mean that it is true. Study the Bible after class. Make sure what the teacher said lines up with God's Word. If something seems to be wrong, talk with your Mom or Dad about it.

Then what does verse 22 tell us? Stay away from bad stuff! Watching bad stuff, listening to bad stuff, doing bad stuff – the word **evil** describes the things that really frustrate Jesus. They bother Jesus because they can hurt you (inside your heart).

The "fuel" for the Holy Spirit's fire is: being kind to others, learning and obeying the Bible (being careful to study it yourself) and making sure that you do what pleases Jesus.

The "oxygen" for the Spirit's fire is being happy you know God, praying and thanking God.

---

[38] Prophecy is telling what God is saying. Today we have what God said written for us in the Bible.

[39] 1 Thessalonians 5:21 "Test everything" – check it out by comparing it to the Bible.

I'm praying for you – I want you to always keep the Holy Spirit's fire burning.

CHAPTER 9
Fill up – and don't grieve

We've already talked about being filled with the Holy Spirit – do you remember? It was in lesson four and I will come back to that later.

Have you ever had a friend who wouldn't listen to you? A friend who didn't care what you thought, and didn't care if they made you feel bad? *I know that kid wouldn't be your friend for long! Who needs friends like that?*

The Holy Spirit lives in us – he is here to be our teammate as we live for Jesus. With the Holy Spirit's strength, we are certain to win! The best teammates are often good friends. As we keep following Jesus, we will grow in our appreciation for the Holy Spirit and learn to depend on him. Yes, you could say we are friends with him.

So we come to our first scripture. I'm glad you already had your Bible ready. Go ahead and read Ephesians 4:30. You may not recognize some of these words or know their meaning; that's ok – we'll talk about them now. To grieve means to be sad because we lost something or someone. It can be as simple as breaking one of your favorite toys, or tearing clothes that you really liked; and it can be as hard as having a pet die. We're talking really, really sad.

This verse tells us that it is possible for you and me to make the Holy Spirit really sad. We should be super-careful that we don't do that! How do we make the Holy Spirit sad? I think it would be good to read this verse in **context** – do you remember what that means?[40] The context here is Ephesians 4:25-5:2 (Did you notice? We didn't stop at the end of a chapter. Sometimes the idea keeps going ... don't let chapter breaks stop you from reading and checking it out.)

There is a lot in here about the attitudes we have and the words we say. Let's add them up:
1)   Don't lie.
2)   Don't hold a grudge. Don't go to sleep when you are still mad. (Maybe you ought to check with your Mom or Dad if you don't know what that means.)
3)   Instead of taking – learn to give.

---

[40] "To read the verses before and after to see what the writer is talking about."

4)	Make sure you say things that help people, rather than saying things to hurt them.

5)	Get rid of your bad attitudes.[41]

6)	Forgive others like God forgave you. That's why you are a Christian – because Jesus died so your sins could be forgiven!

7)	Imitate God – especially in the way he shows love to all kinds of people.

Did you know there is a verse in the Old Testament that talks about "grieving" the Holy Spirit?

There sure is, and it is talking about God's people, the Israelites.[42] God did kind and loving things for them, and I'm sorry to say, they didn't care. They disobeyed the Lord and had a bad attitude about it. This made the Holy Spirit really sad and he stopped helping them for a while.

I want you to really think about this: Jesus loves us. He wants what is best for us and showed that by going to the cross so we can be forgiven. Jesus' asks

_____

[41] Bitterness is a bad attitude because we're mad about something all the time. Rage – throwing a fit. Anger – people may not see it, but we are mad and do things we know will bother them. Brawling – that's fighting! Slander is saying mean things about someone. Malice – that word covers all bad attitudes.

[42] Isaiah 63:10. The context begins at 63:7

us to care about people the same way he cares about you and me. The Holy Spirit is ready to help us. When we have a bad attitude, when we say mean things or lie – we are rebelling against what Jesus wants for us. This is a way that we can grieve the Holy Spirit.

I know it can be hard sometimes, especially when things don't go the way you want them to; but don't do it! Don't grieve the Holy Spirit. He is the one who makes you special for God. You need his help. When things are bothering you, cooperate with the Holy Spirit. Turn to Jesus for help instead of turning on your bad attitude.

I already told you about the command "be filled with the Spirit."[43] Did you remember? Did you go back and check? Our life is like a house, we can let the Holy Spirit go anywhere he wants to in our "house" or we can lock him in a closet and only let him go with us to church or places like that.

When I teach about the Holy Spirit in Africa, I talk about locking him in a closet and only taking him to church. They think that is really funny. But sadly, it is also true. Many Christians do not really want the

---

[43] Ephesians 5:18

Holy Spirit to change the way they live. I am really happy that you don't think that way.

I want you to notice the **context** again (Ephesians 5:15-6:9). It does talk about things we do at church – like singing. It talks about being wise[44] and doing the Lord's will. But the context also talks about how to obey your parents! It talks about how to treat your boss (or your teacher).[45] It tells us how married people should care for each other.

Living for Jesus is not just about church; it is about the way we live every part of our lives! The Holy Spirit lives in us to help us. He can't help if we lock him up. I hope you have already begun praying each day, "Lord, fill me with the Holy Spirit."

If you ask, he will answer.[46] If you cooperate, the Holy Spirit will help you in every part of your life.

---

[44] Wise is being smart in how we live, not just smart because we know the answers to questions. Proverbs 1:7

[45] We aren't slaves. But many things they are taught here would apply to going to work or school… think about it that way.

[46] Luke 11:13

Jesus says when we obey him we will experience his joy.[47] This is what I want for you.

---

[47] John 15:9-12

CHAPTER 10

The Holy Spirit helps us tell others about Jesus

We have talked a lot about the Holy Spirit. I hope that you know the Holy Spirit better now and you want to let him work with you. He wants to help you and me to follow Jesus.

There are a few more things that I want you to understand about the Holy Spirit. This one you know personally. Try to remember what you were thinking and how you felt while you were deciding whether or not you should follow Jesus and be baptized.

You see, the Holy Spirit was working in your mind and heart. He was making you think a lot about God's Son and showing you that it made sense for you to give your life to Christ. That is one of the Holy Spirit's jobs, he invites people to follow Jesus.

I'm so glad that you get your Bible out right away. You know that we're going to look at the scriptures, don't you? On the night before Jesus died, in John 16, he said the Spirit would convict the world of their sin.[48] When you began thinking a lot about Jesus, did you think about how you had done bad things and that you needed to be forgiven? I know I did! (Do you remember how old I was when I was baptized?[49])

Did you think about the fact that the Bible tells the truth about Jesus: First that he died for our sins and rose from the dead? Then that when Jesus comes back it will be a surprise (no one knows the time), and that it makes more sense to follow him than to live for the devil? Do you know who was putting those thoughts into your brain? You are right. The Holy Spirit was doing it.

He didn't just do that with you and me. He is busy doing it with all sorts of people, all around the world. There is something else you need to understand. **The Holy Spirit wants to team up with us to help us tell others about Jesus.**

When we look at the book of Acts, we find him helping Christians to meet people who need to learn about Jesus. One time, God wanted a man from

---

[48] John 16:7-11

[49] Eleven. I was baptized on February 7, 1968

Ethiopia[50] to learn about Jesus. This man had a really important job in the government, he was the Treasurer. He was so interested in the true God that he traveled to Jerusalem to worship and he owned a hand-copy of the book of Isaiah, in the Old Testament (those were expensive!).[51]

First, an angel sent Philip to a road out in the middle of nowhere. Then the African man came by in his chariot.[52] The Holy Spirit told Philip to run beside the chariot! That must have been a strange sight. As you read this, you will see how Philip told the man about Jesus, and then the African man asked to be baptized. Did you see what happened right after Philip baptized him? What did the Holy Spirit do?

Do you see how involved the Spirit is in helping believers in Jesus to meet other people? Not just any people; we are talking about people who are

---

[50] Ethiopia is a country in Africa. Get a map and look, it is toward the northeast.

[51] Acts 8:26-40

[52] I think you would enjoy seeing what a chariot looked like. You can find one online. This is something you can do with your Mom or Dad.

interested in the Bible and knowing God.[53] Sometimes the Holy Spirit has said, "No, don't go there," so that the gospel will be taken to a place that God has selected.[54] I hope you can see how busy the Spirit is, working so people can learn about Jesus.

I want you to think about something. You know Jesus and you know from the Bible the truth about God. You also know from your experience what it is like to give your life to Christ and follow him. The Holy Spirit wants you to be his partner to tell people about the Lord and invite them to follow, just like you did.[55] Maybe he wants you to talk to your friends; maybe it is someone in your family, or even someone you don't know yet.

The Holy Spirit helps us whenever we are willing to tell others about Jesus. Perhaps it is the other way around; we are helping him![56] He also helps people who are trying to decide whether or not they want to obey the Lord to go ahead and commit to him.[57]

---

[53] Acts 10:19, 20; Acts 11:11-14; Acts 13:1-4

[54] Acts 16:6-10

[55] John 15:26, 27

[56] 1 Thessalonians 1:4, 5; 1 Peter 1:12

[57] 1 Thessalonians 1:6

I know many times that the Holy Spirit will use the Bible to speak to a person's heart and encourage them to come to Christ. That makes a lot of sense, since he wrote the Bible – we will study that next.

"For you have been born again ... through the living and enduring word of God."[58] You see, it is good to tell others the stories and memory verses that you know from the Bible. It will be good for them to hear the Bible words, because God has given them to all of us, so we can find Jesus.

This is something that God considers very important: he wants everyone to have a chance to know about our Lord Jesus and follow him.[59] Jesus told us to go and invite people to follow him.[60] And the Holy Spirit is working with people right now, just like he was with you before you decided to follow Jesus.

You might not ever have to run beside someone's car so you can talk, and you may not go on mission trips like I do. (Maybe someday you will). But I'm

---

[58] 1 Peter 1:23, 24

[59] Acts 17:24-27; 1 Timothy 2:3, 4; 2 Peter 3:9

[60] Matthew 28:18-20

sure that the Holy Spirit is working with someone near you, helping them to think about Jesus. He wants partners to tell them the good news about Jesus. Let's help him!

CHAPTER 11

The Holy Spirit wrote the Bible

When you were little, your Mom and Dad read Bible stories to you. Did you have a favorite story or story book? Many kids go to Bible class at church and learn Bible stories there, too. I bet you learned a lot about Jesus.

There are several great stories from the Old Testament about God, the Father. They tell how he worked to help his people, to teach them and to correct them.

We don't learn very much about the Holy Spirit in those Bible stories, so sometimes people know very little about him. His work may be quieter, more behind the scenes, but it is still very important. That is why I am writing you to teach you about him.

Here is something I want you to think about: the reason we have all those great Bible stories[61] is

---

[61] They really happened, you know. They are not like a fairy tale or Star Wars. They happened at real places, to real people in real history.

because the Holy Spirit made sure that they were put into the Bible. Yes, he wrote the Bible!

The Holy Spirit wrote the Bible in a very special way. He worked carefully in the hearts of men who loved God. He helped them to think about God's truth and encouraged them to write it down so others could read it. The Holy Spirit made sure that their words were God's words.

Let me show you. You have your Bible ready, right? That's great; I knew you would.

Find 2 Peter and the first chapter. It is good if you have already memorized the books of the Bible. That helps you to find places quickly. Don't be embarrassed if you do not find them quickly. Just go to the table of contents in your Bible and you can find the page number.

Did you find 2 Peter chapter one? We will read verses 20 & 21. Read it right now. Do you see what it says?

Prophecy means "speaking for God" or "speaking God's words." There were many prophets in the Old Testament. You have learned about some of them in the Bible stories that you already know. All the books from Isaiah to Malachi are written by prophets.

Look at the verses again. Did the Old Testament prophets make up the words that they said? No way! Who helped them to speak and write God's words? The Holy Spirit – you are right.

Now find Acts 4:24-26. This passage is from a very hard time for the first Christians. The Jewish leaders were being mean to them and threatening to hurt them because they were telling others about Jesus. So they prayed.

In their prayer, they quoted some verses from Psalm 2.[62] But they didn't say, "Psalm 2 says this." What did they say?

They understood that the reason we have Psalm 2, and any Psalm, is because the Holy Spirit gave David and the other psalmists[63] the words to say. There are other places in the New Testament where this idea is repeated.[64]

---

[62] Psalm 2:1, 2

[63] A psalm is a Hebrew song. You call that song-writer a psalmist.

[64] Acts 1:16; Acts 28:25; Hebrews 3:7; Hebrews 10:15-17

Jesus said something interesting about his words. Go ahead and find John 14:25, 26. Jesus is talking to his disciples on the night before he died on the cross. Of course Jesus knew that, and so he was talking to them about some very, very important things.

Do you see what Jesus promised here? How would his disciples[65] be able to remember all the things he had taught and told them? You saw it right away, didn't you? Jesus promised that the Holy Spirit would remind them!

So, we know that the Holy Spirit wrote the Old Testament and helped the disciples of Jesus to write the gospels.[66] What about the New Testament? Do you think the Holy Spirit had anything to do with the rest of the New Testament?

Let's check it out. Look at John 16:12-15. In verse thirteen, what does Jesus tell them the Holy Spirit will do? Jesus told his disciples that the Holy Spirit would guide them into how much truth? Yes, that's right, __all__ truth.

---

[65] Disciple means: student, follower and friend.

[66] **Matthew, Mark** wrote for Peter, **Luke** interviewed many disciples, **John**

In verse fifteen, he says it in another way. The Holy Spirit would communicate God's truth to Jesus' disciples. Jesus was saying that we can depend on the words we read in the New Testament, that they will be from God.[67]

The Holy Spirit worked carefully to make sure that the Bible was written so we could have the true and accurate words of God. You and I have the privilege of reading these words.

When we read and pay attention, we are listening to the Holy Spirit. That is why I told you that reading, thinking about and obeying the Bible are important parts to "setting our minds on what the Spirit desires."[68] This same attitude about the Bible is true when we talk about planting (sowing) to please the Spirit.[69]

---

[67] 1 Corinthians 7:10; 7:40 – Paul was not with Jesus when Jesus said the words we find in John 14 & 16, but he did spend a lot of time with Jesus later. (Galatians 1:11, 12, 15-18) Paul insists here that he is speaking the word of the Lord. Peter agrees and says so in 2 Peter 3:15, 16.

[68] Romans 8:5, 6

[69] Galatians 6:7, 8

The Bible is a letter from God to us. Because we love God, we will want to read it, learn it, obey it and then tell others about it. I am so grateful that the Holy Spirit wrote it for you and me.

CHAPTER 12

The Holy Spirit will help you to be a good helper

Have you ever helped someone, not because you had to but because you <u>wanted</u> to do it?

Maybe you helped your mom or dad with work around the house. Maybe you helped at church, like a time when you took care of some little kids. And you might have given someone directions or helped a friend to understand their school work.

Whenever I help someone, I have a good feeling inside me. It is not easy to explain, but I think you know the feeling, too. It is a happy and satisfying feeling. It says to my heart, "You did something good!" Even if I am very tired, this good feeling makes all the hard work of helping worth it.

Have you had that type of feeling when you have helped someone? I hope you have already felt it and that you felt it this week. You will more and more as you grow up.

The Holy Spirit has moved into us to help us live for Jesus.

I am sure that you already know this – *a big part of living for Jesus is helping other people*: your family, people in your church, your friends and even people you do not know.

The Holy Spirit has come to help us be very good helpers. In fact, the Bible tells us that the Holy Spirit gives us each at least one gift. Now this is not a birthday present. The gift that he gives you is the ability to help other people in a special way.

What I just told you sounds kind of weird. The Holy Spirit gives us the gift, but its real purpose is for us to give to someone else! That doesn't sound fair, does it? It makes sense when we think about that special good feeling we have when we help someone. You see, when we help, the person we help feels good and we feel good. This is good for everyone.

There are places in the Bible where we can see lists of the types of gifts the Spirit gives to us because we follow Jesus.[70]

---

[70] Romans 12:3-8; 1 Corinthians 12:8-11; Ephesians 4:11-13; 1 Peter 4:10, 11; Exodus 35:30-35

But right now, I want you to think with me more about, "Why do I get a gift?" than about, "What gift am I going to get?"

Both Paul and Peter wrote about this to Christians like you and me. They were talking to people who wanted to please Jesus. *And we both know that the Holy Spirit actually helped them to write, don't we?*

Paul said, "A spiritual gift is given to each of us so we can help each other."[71]

Peter said, "God has given each of you a gift ... Use them well to serve one another."[72]

Jesus expects you and me to love him with all of our hearts; **and to obey him.** Jesus told us to love others, especially those who belong to Jesus.[73] One of the best ways to show our love is to be willing to help.

When someone is sad and we are willing to listen to her, hug her and maybe even cry with her, we are helping.

---

[71] 1 Corinthians 12:7 (NLT)

[72] 1 Peter 4:10 (NLT)

[73] John 15:9-12

When someone is discouraged – when he is disappointed because he lost something or failed at something – when we encourage him, we are helping (ask your Mom or Dad about some ways you can encourage others.)

When someone needs money, and we give her some from our allowance, we are helping.

When we teach someone something we have learned from the Bible, we are helping.

There are other special ways to help. What you and I need to do is practice helping; that way we will learn what we are really good at and how we can best help others. The Holy Spirit is ready to make you a very good helper.

I want to remind you of something that Jesus said. We haven't looked up a Bible verse in this chapter, until now; go ahead and find Acts 20:35 in your Bible. Paul tells what Jesus said at the end of that verse.

Read Jesus' words. Do you know what blessed means? It means that good things happen to you.

Do you like getting presents for your birthday and Christmas? I do. Do you like it when your grandparents give you something you've been hoping for a long time? I'm sure you do.

Do you hear what Jesus said here? When do the best things happen to you and me? When we get presents? No, it is when we give.

The context here is about giving money, but there are other things we can give:

You can give time to help. Or you can take time to listen or care about someone. Each of these is a way to give. You do not have to wait until you are older; you belong to Jesus right now. The Holy Spirit lives inside you.

Jesus is ready to do good things for you when you give and the Holy Spirit is ready to make you a very good helper and giver.

I am excited about this. It will be fun to learn about all the ways that you help other people. This will happen as you team up with the Holy Spirit.

CHAPTER 13

The Holy Spirit works in a different way now than he did in the Old Testament

What I want to talk with you about right now can be confusing, but I think you are old enough to understand it. You have already experienced some of this in your school work.

In preschool and kindergarten, which subjects do they teach little kids? ABC's or verbs and pronouns? Geometry or shapes? Numbers or long division? These are not hard questions, are they? Why do you teach school subjects in this way? You are so right; you teach basics and build on them. The goal is to truly understand a subject, so you have to start with simple things first.

The same is true with the way that God teaches his people. The Old Testament is sort of like preschool for God's people. It is all true and we can learn good lessons. We learn about God: his power and his character. And we learn about people: how they treat God and each other.

But God does not want his people to stay in preschool. He wants us to grow up and have a good education about God. That is why Jesus came. He came so that we can know about God. More than that, he came so we can know God like we are part of his family.

One thing the Old Testament teaches us is the importance of sacrifice.[74] Unless God's people sacrificed an animal, their sins could not be forgiven. The Jews in the Old Testament sacrificed a lot of animals!

This type of sacrifice was the simple basic type. It was not the permanent plan of God. Instead, it helps us understand Jesus' sacrifice on the cross. He did that one time to pay for all of our sins.[75]

It is not a good idea for you and me to go back to the old way, the elementary way of understanding about sacrifice. God wants us to understand why Jesus died for us, depend on him for our forgiveness and love Jesus with all our hearts. Of course, we show Jesus our love by obeying him.[76]

---

[74] Leviticus 17:11; Hebrews 9:22

[75] Hebrews 9:23-28

[76] John 14:15; John 15:14

Now, it is time to talk about the Holy Spirit. The Holy Spirit also did a lot of work in the Old Testament.[77] He worked in the life of Samson.[78] When a lion attacked Samson, the Bible says the Spirit of the Lord came on him in power and Samson killed the lion with his bare hands!

You see, the Holy Spirit came on Samson, gave him power and then left until another time. This happened with other leaders of Israel in the Book of Judges. The Holy Spirit would come on them and help them to win a battle.

I gave you a lot of scriptures to look up in the footnotes – you can read them as you go through this lesson, or you can read them afterward.

King Saul was another person who experienced the Holy Spirit's power. Once it was to lead God's people into battle[79], and another time – this was earlier in his life – the Spirit took control of him and

---

[77] I will give you some places: Numbers 11:11-17, 24-30 ; Judges 3:10; 6:34; 11:29;

[78] Judges 13:25; 14:6, 19; 15:14; 16:20

[79] 1 Samuel 11:6

made him prophecy.[80] That means he spoke God's words.

But King Saul did not listen to God very well. He was very disobedient. So, the Holy Spirit left him[81]. The Holy Spirit left Saul and worked with David.[82] Do you see how much the Holy Spirit was moving around? He would come and go. He did this to work out God's plans.

This is one time I just have to tell you about. King Saul was jealous of David. David was popular for killing Goliath, for being a good soldier and a good leader. Saul was mad at David and wanted to kill him. One time he and his soldiers chased David and almost had him trapped. Then the Holy Spirit took over! He took control of Saul and made him lay down all day and speak God's words.[83]

Saul was acting out – he was being a bad guy. But that didn't stop the Holy Spirit from doing his work – he just took over. But when that day was over, the

---

[80] 1 Samuel 10:6, 9-11

[81] 1 Samuel 16:14

[82] 1 Samuel 16:13

[83] 1 Samuel 19:23, 24

Spirit was not with King Saul. He just took over that day to protect David.

In the Old Testament, we find the Holy Spirit coming and going. When he came, he gave people power to do special things. But then he would leave until the next time. He didn't stay.

You and I don't live in Old Testament times. We live in New Testament times. Jesus has come and we follow him. Jesus promised that the Holy Spirit would live inside of us,[84] and that he would come to stay! This is exactly what I have been telling you in these lessons.

I want you to remember, too, the Old Testament way is like preschool; it was getting people ready for the really important stuff. Following Jesus is the most important thing. That is what you and I have chosen to do.

Here is where we find a problem. Preschool is fun. But when we grow older, school work can be really hard. A lot of kids would rather play than do the grown up work.

---

[84] John 14:15-17

The Holy Spirit's "grown up work" is to help us to live for Jesus. He has come into our lives to teach us to obey Jesus and live like him. So the Holy Spirit wants to help us to stop doing, thinking and saying bad things. This is tough stuff.

It sounds like more fun to have super powers and beat bad guys like Samson did. Some people think it would be really exciting to have the Holy Spirit take control of them like he did with King Saul. *But Samson and Saul did not make God happy with the way they lived.* They had power, but they did not have the character of Jesus.

In preschool times (Old Testament), the Holy Spirit came and left. In our grown up life, the Holy Spirit comes into us to stay with us. That has been God's plan all along.[85]

Some adults who are Christians do not understand this. They expect the Holy Spirit to come and leave. When they are in church, they pray for the Spirit to come. There are some really nice songs about the Holy Spirit that invite him to come.

---

[85] Ezekiel 36:24-27; John 7:37-39; Romans 8:9-11; Romans 8:15, 16

The Holy Spirit lives in me and lives in you. So if we go to church, where is he? Do we need to invite him to come? No, because he already came with us.

I want you to think about this. If you understand it well, it will help you to cooperate with the Holy Spirit and live well for Jesus.

Remember always, the Holy Spirit is in your life. He won't leave you. He came in to stay and to help you when you live for Jesus. He is the best friend and helper you will ever have because he is God.

I am praying for you. I pray that you will really be good at working with the Holy Spirit.

CHAPTER 14

The Holy Spirit wants you to follow Jesus' example

Get your Bible ready. I hope you are taking time to look at the places in the Bible that I have mentioned to you. It is always best to see things with your own eyes.

Right after Jesus was baptized. The Holy Spirit led him somewhere – you can find this in the fourth chapter of Matthew.[86] Read Matthew 4:1, 2. I'm going to ask you a few questions:

- Where did the Holy Spirit lead Jesus?
- What happened to Jesus there?
- Who came to talk to Jesus?

Here we go again! This is another difficult place in the Bible. Why would the Holy Spirit take Jesus to a place where the devil would come to tempt him? Why would Jesus go without eating for over a month? The Bible says that Jesus was hungry. Do you think you would be hungry, too?

---

[86] We also can see it in Mark 1:12, 13 and in Luke 4:1, 2

This is a very important question – why would the Holy Spirit lead Jesus into a place where he would be tempted? Jesus taught us to pray, "… lead us not into temptation …".[87] Why was Jesus "… *led into the desert to be tempted by the devil?*" Does that seem fair to you?

The Holy Spirit made sure that we could read about what happened to Jesus when he was in the desert. He wants us to watch how Jesus stood up to the devil when Satan tried to get him to disobey his Father.

The Bible tells us that Jesus was *"tempted in every way that we are; but he never sinned."*[88]

What does tempt mean? Do you know? It is being invited or being dared to do something that is wrong. The devil does this, but we can't see him. People can tempt us, too. Sometimes even our friends do.

A temptation is like a commercial on TV. Do you watch the commercials or do you change channels? Why do companies spend so much money to put commercials on TV? They want you to buy their

---

[87] Matthew 6:13; Luke 11:4

[88] Hebrews 4:15

video games, or food, or clothes or toys. So they make you think it's the best game ever! The food looks great and everyone is having a good time eating it, right?

The devil has commercials for us. He doesn't use the TV. He talks to our minds. Sometimes he hides behind people as they tell us or show us that we can have fun doing something that God doesn't like. Always remember, Satan does not care if we have a good time. Instead, he wants us to be separated from God.

That is exactly what he was trying to do when he tempted Jesus! You and I can't hide from temptation. We must deal with it. So Jesus faced the same problem that we do – and we can see how he won! I want you to pay careful attention here, because you and I need to learn how to win this, too.

Go ahead and read Matthew 4:1-11. Look for the three things that the devil suggested to Jesus. These temptations were especially for Jesus. What did Satan want him to do? Let's look at each one:

> 1.   He told Jesus to turn stones into bread. That only works for Jesus! I can't change stones into bread (If I could, I would probably

make them into cinnamon rolls!). Can you change stones into bread? It is not a temptation for us – but is was for Jesus. The devil invited Jesus to be <u>selfish</u> with his power. That would have been a sin for Jesus.

2.   Satan took Jesus to the highest place on the temple in Jerusalem. He dared Jesus to jump and told him the angels would catch him. Does it sound like fun to you? Some kids would have a great time jumping if they knew they wouldn't get hurt. Others are afraid of heights. Why would this be bad for Jesus to do?

The people where Jesus lived had been taught from the Old Testament that the Messiah[89] would appear suddenly in the temple.[90] They were taught that he was going to jump from the sky and land in the

---

[89] Messiah is the Hebrew word for "anointed one." The person chosen by God to be the king of Israel, like David was in 1 Samuel 16:12, 13 . What was poured on David? Oil. Pouring oil on someone is called anointing them. Actually, kings and prophets and priests were chosen this way. The "Anointed One" was the most special person who would ever come to Israel. Remember – the Hebrew word for this is Messiah. The Greek word is Christos or Christ.

[90] Malachi 3:1. (Jesus did appear in the temple suddenly – John 2:12-16)

temple! So they were all looking for the Messiah to come that way and they were ready to follow him immediately.

If Jesus had listened to Satan, when he landed he would have been very <u>popular</u>. Satan was saying, "See, Jesus, people will follow you and you won't have to die on the cross." The cross was God's plan for Jesus. To avoid God's plan would be disobedient. It would be wrong.

Is it wrong to be popular? No, not necessarily. But if you want to be popular more than you want to obey God, it will lead to big trouble in your life. You will find yourself doing things that do not please God.

3.   The devil offered Jesus all sorts of money, fun stuff and power if Jesus would do something; do what? Worship the devil! Jesus would have to turn his back on the Father and <u>be unfaithful</u>.

The evil one[91] had a couple more tricks up his sleeve. Do you see how he started talking to Jesus? Look in verse 3. He said, "If you are the Son of God ..." Satan knew Jesus when Jesus was in heaven

---

[91] That's what the apostle John called Satan – 1 John 5:19

before he came to earth. He knew Jesus was the Son of God. Why did he say that?

He wanted Jesus to question himself. He wanted Jesus to be anxious, because he was away from the Father and because life here is not easy. He wanted Jesus to start thinking, "Maybe God doesn't like me or accept me." He does something similar for us. Satan knows that if we think God doesn't like us we won't care about what pleases God.

Next, the devil came when Jesus was really, really hungry and weak. How long had it been since Jesus ate anything? How many weeks is that (almost)? Satan came after Jesus in his weakness. He does the same thing with us. He will invite us to do bad things when we're tired, or hungry, or mad. We need to remember this and be ready.

Finally, the evil one told Jesus a memory verse! Do you see it in Matthew 4:6? That is from Psalm 91. The devil reads the Bible; he knows it very well. He is willing to tell us memory verses or hide behind other people giving memory verses. But always remember, Satan twists the verses to say things that God did not intend. He tries to trick us with the Bible!

How can we beat the devil? We need to know the Bible as well as Jesus did!

What I'm going to tell you now, I learned when I was 15 years old. I thought of this myself while I was reading right here, in Matthew 4. This was not the first time I read it; I have gone to church my whole life and read my Bible many times. But that was the time when this really made sense to me.

First, I noticed how Jesus talked back to Satan after each temptation. Did you see that? Look at verses 4, 7 and 10 again. What did Jesus do? He quoted the Bible, he told memory verses to the devil! Each of these verses is from Deuteronomy.[92] Jesus knew his Bible very well. He even knew that the devil misused Psalm 91 – so he ignored that. He said the right memory verse.

Next, look and see how Satan responded when Jesus quotes scripture. He changed the subject. He did not argue with Jesus! He tried something else. Then Jesus told him to leave and the devil left. In Luke 4:13, we are reminded that Satan left then, but he was always looking for a way to get Jesus to disobey the Father.

---

[92] Deuteronomy 8:3; 6:16; 6:13

But Jesus never did disobey! Jesus never did anything wrong.[93] Ever.

How did Jesus stop the devil's commercials? How did he say "no?" He quoted Bible verses!

This thought became clear in my mind when I was 15; *"If Jesus, the perfect Son of God, needed to quote scripture to stop the devil, I should do the very same thing."*

So right then, I started. Whenever I know that Satan is showing me a commercial; when he is telling me that disobeying God is fun, I know what to do. I give the evil one a memory verse.

Sometimes he tells me to steal something. Most of the time, he just puts a thought in my mind. I tell him, "No Satan, because the Bible says 'You shall not steal.'"[94] When I quote the verse, the devil leaves me alone.

Now for me, he comes back about five minutes later with the same temptation. But I know what to

---

[93] 1 John 3:4-8 (look at verse 5)

[94] Exodus 20:15. Think about this – cheating on school work or tests is stealing answers.

do – I say the verse again. And he goes away. I don't know why, but he normally bothers me three times. I'm ready; I say the verse and then we are finished for a while.

I have been doing this for a long time now, with all sorts of different temptations. There are verses in the Bible to quote for each one. It works. Satan does not like for me to quote scripture to him and he leaves me alone. It will work for you, too.[95]

The Holy Spirit knows that we need help and strength to learn how to stop doing bad things – the things that don't please God. He lives inside of you and me to help us.

The Holy Spirit led Jesus into the desert to face the devil so that we could learn a very important lesson from him. Jesus taught us how to push Satan's temptations aside and say "no."

This is not something that only Jesus could do. You have the Bible, too. You can memorize verses

---

[95] You can find the verses yourself, if you want to. But if you have trouble finding one, ask for help. Your parents will be willing to help. Or you can ask a teacher at church. Don't wait to get started. Get your verses ready. Memorize them and get ready to say them when you are tempted.

and quote them, too. You will be tempted, too – the devil does it to us every day. Get ready to fight back. Begin saying verses back to the evil one.

I have been doing it since I was 15. I know how powerful the Word of God is. I want you to learn the power of God early in your life. I am praying for you.

CHAPTER 15
How can the Holy Spirit be God?

I asked this question much earlier: How can the Holy Spirit be God? He is not the Father or Jesus, the Son of God?

I told you then we would talk about it later; well, it is time to talk. This idea is called "the trinity."[96]The trinity is very difficult to understand. Some people take advantage of this to teach things that are not true. Others refuse to accept it as truth about our God.

Most just say, "I don't understand this, so I don't want to think about it." If we stop trying to understand God, we will miss out on a lot of good things that God has for us.

So get your Bible. Oh, you already have it here; good! Find Acts chapter 5. In this chapter we learn

---

[96] The word "trinity" is not in the Bible; but the idea of God being one God, yet three persons is described in the Bible. The word the New Testament writers use is "godhead." The word godhead is translated that way in the KJV – it is found in Romans 1:20 and Colossians 2:9

about a husband and wife who lied about money they gave to the church. That is not a good idea, and God chose to punish them. You can read the whole story later; please read 5:1-4 for me right now.

Now I have a quiz for you. In verse three, who does Peter say Ananias lied to?

In verse four, Peter said, "... you have not lied to men but to _____" (fill in this blank). So when a person lies to the Holy Spirit, he is lying to God.

Some people think the Holy Spirit is like a ghost[97] or he is some kind of power. Can you lie to electricity? No, you can only lie to a person.

There are other places in the Bible I want you to see. Let's start with Mark 1:9-11. When you were baptized, did anyone take pictures or video? I imagine they did. It is always a very special occasion when people are baptized.

---

[97] The King James Version (KJV) was translated in the 1600's. It calls the Holy Spirit – "Holy Ghost." Some people have decided from this that the Holy Spirit is just some kind of spiritual thing, but not God. They made a mistake because they didn't understand that language changes over many years. That is why it is good to have a Bible translation that was done near the time you were growing up.

Right here, we see a family "video." When Jesus is baptized, who can we see? Yes, Jesus is there. And the Holy Spirit, right? He comes from heaven in the form of a dove – but the Bible says this was the Holy Spirit. Then we hear a voice. Whose voice is it? It is God the Father because he calls Jesus his Son. So the Father, Son and Holy Spirit are all in the "video" when Jesus was baptized.

You are really close to Matthew 28:18-20, so back up to that now. Verse 19 is about baptism, too. We are supposed to invite people to follow Jesus – that is what "making disciples" is about. Then, when they decide that they truly want to follow Jesus and learn from him, we are to baptize them. Jesus told us that we are to baptize them in a special way, do you see it? Baptize them in the name of the Father, the Son and the Holy Spirit.[98]

Right here, I need to tell you something that the Greek language says. Remember, the New Testament was written first in Greek. Jesus did not say to baptize in the name(s) of the Father, Son and Holy

---

[98] Baptizing in the name does not necessarily mean that we have to say those names when we baptize. It really means that we are baptizing them by the authority of God (the Father, Son and Holy Spirit). In other words, we baptize those who want to follow Jesus because God said to do it.

Spirit; he said to baptize in the name. One name. Not three names, but one name. Why only one name? Because there is only one God.[99]

Jesus taught us this truth. He is God, the Father is God and the Holy Spirit is just like Jesus.[100]

How can <u>one</u> God be <u>three</u> people? I will not tell you that this is easy to understand. But you and I have studied this right now, and the Bible is clear that the Father, Son and Holy Spirit are God.

Some Bible teachers have used different things to show that God can be three and still one. One way is to look at an egg. Do you like eggs? I do. An egg has a yoke and a white part; and it has its own container! Yes, the shell. They are three different things, but one egg.

Other teachers have said that water best explains this truth about God. Water is liquid. But sometimes it is a solid. When does that happen? And if you heat water up to a boil, where does some of it go? That's

---

[99] Mark 12:29-31; 2 Corinthians 13:14; Ephesians 2:18 – "for through him (Jesus) we both have access to the Father by one Spirit."

[100] John 14:15-17. We talked about this in chapter 2. You may want to go back there and see how I explained it.

right, it becomes steam or water vapor – a gas. So water can be three different things while all being water. Your parents can explain to you about times when all three parts of water are around in the same place.

These ideas kind of help us to see that there are things that can be three, yet one; but they don't completely help us understand about God. We will need to admit that God lives outside of our experience in the world, so it will be difficult for us to explain about him with science or math.

I want to tell you about something that helps me. If it helps you, I am glad.

We need to talk about dimensions. A line _____ has length. That is one dimension.

I bet you have learned about this in school. A rectangle has two dimensions: length and height.

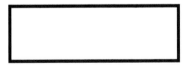

Whatever we draw on paper or a white board has how many dimensions? Two.

How many dimensions does a cube have? Three. Length, height and now width (depth or thickness).

Now, I need you to use your imagination. Imagine with me that we live on a white board. We will only know two dimensions. Length & height.

Pretend someone comes and says to us, "I just made a great discovery! There are really three dimensions! There is depth!"

We would say, "What?" "Are you crazy?" "Everyone living on this white board knows that there is no such thing as depth or cubes!" "We only have length and height."

He would say, "But listen, I have been to a different place. There is a bigger universe than what is here on our white board. Believe me, there really are cubes out there!"

This seems a little silly, doesn't it? I mean, you know there are cubes because you used to play with blocks when you were little. What I want you to think about is the idea of dimensions.

It is outside of our natural experience, but Jesus came here from heaven. And Jesus says that there is another dimension where God can be three persons, but still one God.

We can understand Jesus because we have learned stories about him and seen pictures that people have drawn. He was a human being like us when he walked on the earth. You need to know something that the Bible says about Jesus – *he lived in heaven before he came here.*[101]

That's right. Jesus lived in heaven with the Father and Holy Spirit. They created the world together. At the right time, Jesus came to earth and was born.

Like I said, we can understand Jesus. We can understand the Father, too. We can because we each have a father, or know someone who does. We often call the Father – "God."

These are difficult ideas, but I really think that you are old enough to consider them. The word God can be a name. It can also be an adjective, or a way to describe someone. God has always lived – there has never been a time when he was not there. God can

---

[101] John 1:1-4; John 1:14; John 1:10; John 1:18; John 8:23; John 17:5; Colossians 1:16; Colossians 2:9

create. God can be everywhere at the same time and God is all powerful.

When I tell you that Jesus is God, I don't mean that Jesus is the Father. I mean that Jesus made us and Jesus has always been there. He is all powerful. The Father is God, too.

Also, the Holy Spirit is God. He created us.[102] He is all powerful. He is everywhere at the same time.

Some people say, "Ok, but the Holy Spirit is different, he is a spirit." Jesus told us that God is spirit.[103] "Yes, but the Holy Spirit is different, he lives inside of us." True, but that is his 'job.'

Find John 14:15-17. What did Jesus say he would do when we obey him? He, that's Jesus, would ask the Father to send who? Another Counselor. Do you remember from chapter 2 – what does that word 'another' mean in the Greek language? *Another of the same kind.* Who is this Counselor? The Spirit of truth. That's another name for the Holy Spirit.

---

[102] Genesis 1:2

[103] John 4:24

Where will the Holy Spirit live? "... <u>with</u> you and <u>in</u> you."

This whole idea of our God being <u>three</u>, but <u>one</u> is still very hard to understand. I have tried to explain it the best I know how, and I have thought about it for a very, very long time. Still, it is not easy.

It comes down to this: Jesus told all of us about this and I believe Jesus. I know that you believe him, too. Jesus always tells the truth, so we can trust him. Even if we can't understand everything about it, we know we can trust Jesus.

Know this: the God who made you, loves you. His Son came to earth to show you how to live – he did it perfectly. He died on the cross in your place so your sins can be forgiven.

God, the Holy Spirit, lives inside of you because you love Jesus. You showed Jesus that you love him when you obeyed him. And you show him that you love him every day because you want to obey him.

Keep showing Jesus that you love him. The Holy Spirit is here to help you love and obey Jesus. I am glad that you are learning to rely on the Spirit's help.

CHAPTER 16

I want you to understand how much power you really have

Have you lived in the same place your whole life, or have you moved around? I have moved a lot. Paul, the apostle, lived in many places, too. He went on some long mission trips where he would move from place to place.

Paul stayed in one location for a little more than two years. It is a city called Ephesus.[104] He helped a lot of people there learn the truth about Jesus.[105] A whole lot of people obeyed Jesus, just like we did.

Later, when Paul moved away, he wanted to tell these people that he loved them and he wanted to encourage them to keep following Jesus. So he wrote

---

[104] It is in the country called Turkey. This place was called Asia in Bible times.

[105] You can learn about Paul's first time in Ephesus in Acts 19.

them a letter. It is in your New Testament. I want you to look in the table of contents of your Bible. Now, look for a book that might be written to people from Ephesus.[106] Did you find it? Good, now go ahead and find the book in your Bible.

Paul starts this letter by telling the Christians all the very special things that God has done for us. That is the context for what comes next.

Next, he says," I am so excited about you! I have learned that you trust Jesus and that you love each other." (When we follow Jesus it is natural for us to love others who follow Jesus – we are all part of the same family. God's family.)

He said, "I couldn't help myself. I keep praying for you!" Normally, we think about praying for people when something is wrong, don't we? When someone is sick or in an accident, we want to pray for them. That is good. But it is also good to pray for people when things are going well.

This is Paul's prayer. It is Ephesians 1:15-21. You may want to read it in your Bible, too.

---

[106] I live in Texas. We are called Texans. What would a person from Ephesus be called?

> **15** I have heard about your faith in the Lord Jesus. I have also heard about your love for all God's people. That is why **16** I have not stopped thanking God for you. I always remember you in my prayers. **17** I pray to the God of our Lord Jesus Christ. God is the glorious Father. I keep asking him to give you the wisdom and understanding that come from the Holy Spirit. I want you to know God better. **18** I pray that you may understand more clearly. Then you will know the hope God has chosen you to receive. You will know that what God will give his holy people is rich and glorious. **19** And you will know God's great power. It can't be compared with anything else. His power works for us who believe. It is the same mighty strength **20** God showed. He showed this when he raised Christ from the dead. God seated him at his right hand in his heavenly kingdom. **21** There Christ sits far above all who rule and have authority. He also sits far above all powers and kings.
>
> **Ephesians 1:15-21 NIRV**

He started by saying, "I am always thanking God for you." It is important to thank God; yes, we should thank him for the good things we have. But even more, we need to thank him for people: your parents, your grandparents and your brothers and sisters.

Our family is bigger than that (yes, we have cousins ...). Remember what I said just said? We are part of God's family; so everyone who loves Jesus is a brother or sister of yours! Wow, we have a BIG family! It is important that we thank God for our spiritual family, too.

Next, he prayed that God would give them a very special present. This is found in verse 17. What is the present? The ability to know God better and better. Who is going to help us with this? Do you see? The Holy Spirit will.

Now in verse 18, Paul says something that sounds kind of weird. He prays that the "eyes of our hearts may be enlightened." What? Everyone knows that hearts don't have eyes! If they did, they wouldn't be able to see much because our hearts are stuck behind ribs and skin.

This is important to understand. When the Bible uses the term – heart – it is not usually talking about your blood pump or Valentine's Day cards. It is talking about the real you, deep down inside: the part of you that thinks, and feels things like anger or joy or sadness. It is the part of you that is in a good mood or bad mood or has an attitude. The real you. You are right, it doesn't have physical eyes; but the real you can 'see,' or understand.

That is why the scripture box I gave you says in verse 18, "I pray that you may understand more clearly." In other words, a light will switch on inside of us, and we won't be in the dark any more about things that God gives us.

Paul prayed that you and I could understand three things. The first two[107] are about the good things that God has planned for us. The third one is found in verse 19 – I want you to see this.

He prayed that those who believe Jesus would know the power available to us. Look carefully. Is this just a little bit of power? The Greek word translated 'power' here is 'dunamis.'[108] We have an English word that comes from this; it is dynamite. How much power does dynamite have?

We have a lot of power, too! The power God used to raise Jesus from the dead!

How much did Jesus suffer before he died? A lot. How badly was he beaten? How much did he bleed? He was terribly abused, then he died. He was buried before 6 o'clock on Friday evening.

He rose from the dead around sunrise on Sunday morning. How much power did it take to give life to

---

[107] Found in 5:18 – hope and that we have a rich inheritance.

[108] Pronounced doo-nah-mees.

Jesus' dead body? More power than any superhero you have ever heard about!

You and I have the same power as God used when he raised Jesus from the dead! We do.[109]

The Holy Spirit was involved in raising Jesus from the dead. Where does the Spirit live now? Inside you, inside me and inside everyone who loves and obeys Jesus.

You may not feel like you have power, but you do. That is why Paul prayed we could understand, that the 'light' would come on inside of us. I will pray that for you, too.

You have the ability to live for Jesus and obey him. You have the strength to do what Jesus wants you to do; even when it is hard.

You have the power to tell the devil "No" when he tempts you; especially when you quote Bible verses.

You have the strength to obey your Mom and Dad and to stop yourself from being mean to your brother or sister. This is not because you are tough, but

---

[109] Romans 8:9-11; Romans 1:1-4

because God has given you his power – the Holy Spirit is right there, inside of you, helping you with his might.

You have the ability to do special things for Jesus; serving others and helping some people to learn the truth about Jesus.

You are a very special person in this world, because God lives inside of you and he has given his power to you. *The same power he used when he raised Jesus from the dead.*

Learn to cooperate with the Holy Spirit. Be a good team player. Learn the plays; they are in your Bible. Practice obeying Jesus. Don't ever quit Jesus' team.

Ask God to help you really understand what he has given you and how to use his power in a way that will please him.

I know you will do very special things for Jesus. I am so glad that you are learning how to depend on the Holy Spirit to help you. This makes me very happy.

CPSIA information can be obtained
at www.ICGtesting.com
Printed in the USA
LVHW021615210720
661198LV00003B/310

9 781684 111039